Don't Stay Broken

A JOURNEY TO BECOMING A WHOLE PERSON

Jenene Mitchell-Blackwood

DON'T STAY BROKEN. Copyright © 2023. Jenene Mitchell-Blackwood. All Rights Reserved.

No rights claimed for public domain material, all rights reserved. No part of this publication may be reproduced, stored in a retrieval system, or transmitted in any form or by any means, electronic, mechanical, photocopying, recording, scanning, or otherwise, without the prior written permission of the publisher. Violation may be subject to civil or criminal penalties.

ISBN: 978-1-958404-71-3 (paperback)

Printed in the United States of America

FOREWORD

It is easy to feel helpless and overwhelmed in a world where crushed hopes, strained relationships, and severe disappointments seem to be the norm. However, I implore you, dear reader, to resist giving up. Rather, I extend an invitation to you to set out on a life-changing adventure, led by the deep insight and steadfast hope contained in *Don't Stay Broken*.

The author provides an authentic perspective that reminds us that brokenness does not define us, regardless of the devastation of loss, the agony of betrayal, the wreckage of fear, or the weight of past mistakes you have endured. This book extends an invitation to embrace the transformative power of faith, grounded in the unwavering belief that God's grace is sufficient.

Jenene provides insightful advice on navigating the terrifying waters of brokenness by drawing on both personal experiences and biblical principles. She walks you through the process of accepting vulnerability, letting go of guilt and regret, and fully accepting God's promise of redemption with tenderness and compassion. Within these pages, you will find the tools, encouragement, and truths needed to take those first transformative steps toward wholeness.

Don't Stay Broken serves as a ray of hope and a kind reminder that God's rescuing love is always available to us, no matter how broken we may feel. May the words penned within this book speak to your heart, ignite your faith, and guide you towards a future defined not by brokenness but by our authentic identity found in Christ. May you find solace, strength, and, ultimately, the wholeness you seek.

Minister Nickeisha Smith, JP

TABLE OF CONTENTS

Foreword iii
Preface 7
Who Is This Book For? 7
A Little Background About the Author 9
Introduction 11
Chapter One: Family 13
Chapter Two: Starting my Intimate Journey 15
Chapter Three: Attempting Love A Second Time
.... 19
   The Wedding Planning Disaster 20
   Forsaken Dreams and Identity For The Sake Of Love 21
Chapter Four: God's Intervention 23
   Wedding Called Off 24
   After the Engagement Break-Up 24
Chapter Five: The Goodness of God Does Lead You to Repent 27
Chapter Six: The Journey of Healing Began 29

Chapter Seven: The Road to Marriage—Finally. 33

Chapter Eight: Church Hurt 35

Chapter Nine: Hurt in the Corporate World 41

   The Purpose for the Struggles 42

  Conclusion 47

PREFACE

WHO IS THIS BOOK FOR?

1. People who have been hurt from childhood throughout life and have closed their heart to love.

2. People with negative experiences generally in relationships and life—family, work, church—that has left a scar they struggle to heal from.

3. People who are upset with God because it seems like their life has been filled with negative experiences one after the other.

4. Singles so desperate to be married that they will compromise their dreams, personality and resources to get into a relationship.

5. Engaged persons who are seeing red flags and are afraid to call off the wedding until they are comfortable.

6. Ladies who are worried about their biological clock ticking and find themselves in a state of desperation for marriage/family.

A LITTLE BACKGROUND ABOUT THE AUTHOR

I am a pastor's kid. I grew up in church. They always say there is no perfect family. When parents are who they are, children can process their actions negatively and wind up with low self-esteem and feelings of rejection, which was what happened to me. This was the root of my problem. I had different convictions and wondered sometimes whether I was even saved growing up in a Christian home. I felt rejected by God because I felt like I passed for a bad school; I was the last to be accepted into university and the last to graduate. I was also the last to get a job, and when I did, it was never long term. I kept moving, being back on the road again, seeking another job due to the short-term contracts because permanency was not available. Sighs. You can just imagine someone going through so much hardship; wouldn't they feel like God was never on their side?

What was the purpose of all this struggle?

Sarah Jakes-Roberts said that sometimes we think our messed-up lives disqualify us from being a good minister for God, but those very same messed-up experiences are what God will use to let others know that they are not alone in what they are going through on their journey in life.

Writing this book is an indication of growth in my life as I was always concerned with keeping up an image that I was holy and living for God, maybe because I felt like my unique convictions, which seemed to be so different from my family members, had to align with the status quo so I am not seen as a "black sheep." I feared that if people knew my sins and weaknesses, they would judge me and hold that over my head each time I stand to sing, teach or do something in church. I also thought I could not witness to people who did not yet know God if I had fallen into sin because it would mean I was weak, and God is not powerful enough to keep us.

I have always been an encourager, and it is my hope that in reading this book, persons, especially in the church who are stifled by traditions and suffer things in silence, will be encouraged.

INTRODUCTION

How does one heal from broken relationships when they experience them one after the other, and when they were significant relationships?

This is a good question. Most of my brokenness in life came from hurts and disappointments in family, friendship, and intimate relationships. It all started with family. Just a note as I relay my experience that this was a past occurrence in my life, and thanks be to God, the relationship between me and my family is beautiful now. I share to help someone who may need to know they are not alone and that change is possible with Christ Jesus' influence and impact.

While growing up, one of the persons who should have had my back and given me reassurance in my early years, felt like an enemy and my biggest critic. This affected me in my early teens and led to me feeling insecure, having low self-esteem and low confidence, especially in areas where I was criticized.

CHAPTER ONE

FAMILY

My mother admitted, years after we restored our relationship, that when she had me, she was not ready for the added responsibility. She already had my older brother, who was a year and a few months older. She had plans to live her life and pursue some goals.

I remember growing up with helpers in my pre-teens because of my parents' busy work schedule, but at twelve years, Mom probably felt we should be less dependent, and she should have more freedom to pursue the things she was putting on pause for a while. As a child, I could not understand that frustration but felt the rejection indirectly as I felt like a bother most times. She did not display much patience with me learning things in my time, and it felt like my efforts were never enough.

In my eyes, Mom found fault with what was not done well rather than complimenting what was done well. In our conversations later in life, I realized it was because she did not want to have anything to do after I completed a task, so if I was doing it, I needed to do it well.

CHAPTER TWO

STARTING MY INTIMATE JOURNEY

These experiences with my mom seriously affected my self-image and spilled over into other relationships. I used to be a friendly person and loved people genuinely. As a result, people would be drawn to me and desire a deeper friendship/relationship, but behind the friendliness was a fear that if people saw my weaknesses and faults, they would not like me anymore. So, I kept relationships at "arm's length" and never allowed anyone too close to my heart.

Between high school and university, I distinctly remember three guys I was very good friends with at different points, and the minute they mentioned entering a relationship, I turned down the idea of taking it any further than friendship.

Coming from my foundation relationship with my mom, I felt like I could never live up to expectations and never be good enough to maintain a long-term relationship.

My heart opened to a relationship when I saw my sister dating guys, and she announced that she was engaged. I was satisfied all along that I had my sister with me as company, so I did not bother to seek out a relationship anymore. I started experiencing anxiety, realizing that my one close company was soon to leave the house. I went for counselling as, on the night of the wedding, I saw my sister go off on her honeymoon with her husband.

Shortly after I started opening my heart to relationships, one of my attractions became evident to others in my church circles. Persons said he and I did well together and had chemistry as we were working in ministry together. After some time, he was absent from church for a long period and turned up announcing that he was engaged, smiling with me, and introducing his fiancé. I was like, "Is this guy for real?" He did not even have a conversation about us, so apparently there was nothing happening during that time when he said he liked me. You can imagine the embarrassment I felt knowing that it was publicly seen that we were attracted to each other and then this. I smiled and was courteous, but I was hurting deep down. When I went home, I cried.

After taking a chance at opening my heart to love, this is what happened. I sank back into my shell.

CHAPTER THREE

ATTEMPTING LOVE A SECOND TIME

As I was approaching thirty, I found myself ticking with love again for another guy. He was very active in church and passionate about God. We started dating and getting to know each other more outside of church. My brother and sister were now married years ahead of me, and I was in panic mode. Why was I not married yet, and my biological clock was ticking?

This panic made me turn a blind eye to the many red flags that started to show up in this young man. I hinted that I was ready for marriage, and he proposed. My parents and church family were not excited about this one; they also saw the red flags. His mindset, in many ways seen in his behaviors, needed transformation, although he was passionate about God. He was not able to keep a job and had poor relationships with several people, including persons in authority. His ability to deal with me sharing my dissatisfaction with some circumstances and environments I was in was also poor, as he would react when he went into those spaces. I realized I could not just share anything with him, because he could not handle it in a mature manner.

THE WEDDING PLANNING DISASTER

Despite the many red flags, I allowed my panic mode to get the best of me and sent out the wedding invitations. Throughout the planning, he lost his job, and I still pushed, taking on the cost of the different aspects. I was determined to get married. I did not want to hear God on this one. I was puzzled, feeling rejection from God. I had one question: "Why did You favor my siblings with marriage, and I have been waiting fourteen years since my first sibling got married?" I did not remember in those moments that I closed my heart to love and chased away some potential, plus…(we will hear the plus later).

The signs became clearer that this guy was not the one for me. I dreamt one night that his pretty face became ugly. I knew what that meant. I saw it in his actions. Rather than becoming a better person, he got worse.

FORSAKEN DREAMS AND IDENTITY FOR THE SAKE OF LOVE

He started requesting that I dress and look a certain way that I knew was not me. He met me looking like that, so what caused the sudden dissatisfaction? His motives were not pure. As he grew to know me, I was not the person he would want to marry, but he wanted to hold on for perceived benefits. In speaking about the future, he always talked about his mother and family and wanting a chance to take them overseas so they could have a better life. He thought he could get that by being married to me. Nowhere in his discussion did he talk about his dreams for us.

I lost myself. I tried to look like what he wanted. I forsook my dreams to make this relationship work.
I wanted to attend a friend's wedding overseas. He talked me into saving the funds for investment in our lives, so I canceled that trip. I was disappointed as it was a very good friend and I really wanted to go.

I always said I wanted to do all major studies before I got married so that I could have time to give attention to my family. I placed those studies on hold to help fund the wedding, given that he suddenly lost his job during the wedding plans.

I got my dream of being engaged, but I was unhappy. My self-worth was so low that I was willing to give up who I was to stay in a relationship to make it work.

What was the plus…? The plus was that I was broken and in no position to be in a healthy relationship, but I was too blind to see it.

CHAPTER FOUR

GOD'S INTERVENTION

God had to intervene to save his daughter from messing up her life and making a mistake she would regret for life.

It so happened that a confrontation happened between this guy and a relative of mine when I was present. This showed us that he had an anger issue and built-up rage, and the question was, "If he was alone with me in a space, what would he do to me if he was like that in the presence of all of us?"

God had to show me the serious, abusive nature of the guy I was about to force a marriage with.

WEDDING CALLED OFF

That was the last straw. I could not force a marriage beyond that confrontation. I would be desperate. I would be foolish.

Invitations had gone out to family members, church members, friends, and co-workers. I had to painfully call or message each of them to let them know the wedding was off.

AFTER THE ENGAGEMENT BREAK-UP

I withdrew from my local church and moved out of my parents' house to start my post-degree studies and be closer to school. I decided to pursue the goals I had parked for the sake of a relationship. Though I was going through life, I was depressed. I was angry with God. I was embarrassed. "Why couldn't You make the guy become better rather than worse?" I was glad I had classes on Sunday so I could tell people I could not be in church because I had classes. I was backslidden. I went throughout each day going to school and work and locked up in my house, crying and depressed once I was home.

The wedding was called off in September, and I told a friend that I wanted to leave the country and take a break in December as the wedding would have been in December when I was on vacation.

Even in my brokenness, I had a male minister who was encouraging me, and my ex-fiancé still encouraged me after it broke off, but little did I know that he really had an interest in me. He was meeting an emotional need as my heart was in so much pain. I even came near to having sex because, in that moment, and because of all the support he gave me, I felt an obligation and was afraid to say no, but deep down, there was discomfort. I eventually could not ignore the discomfort I was feeling in my gut. I told him, "I can't do this."

He was now married and was pursuing me as, apparently, he was not receiving satisfaction in his marriage, so he was taking advantage of my vulnerable state in order to meet an unmet need. I realized after this revelation that, again, I was being used for someone's selfish gains and not because I was truly loved. This led to me sinking deeper into more emotional pain and disappointment.

In spite of this experience, another guy came into the picture, and before I knew it, he was in my house, and we were petting and fondling, but, somehow, it could not lead to sex. There was this strong force that came over me every time I was to break my virginity with a guy, and I could not move into the act. It was after talking to him that I managed to shift the mood to playing some music and talking about church (yes, he was a church guy). During that time, he started opening up about his promiscuous lifestyle before becoming a Christian, and he said it was the first he had interacted with a female in such a space and not had sex, but he actually enjoyed our interactions because we were discussing topics and music that we both enjoyed.

CHAPTER FIVE

THE GOODNESS OF GOD DOES LEAD YOU TO REPENT

God showed me that if I had had sex with the married man, I would have been pregnant as my period came sometime after, so I was fertile in that window of time. He also showed me that the promiscuous guy is possibly infected with a sexually transmitted disease (STD), having had so many partners and not being careful in his sex life. God was protecting me. Throughout my prayer-less life, I stopped reading the Bible, and I was upset with God, yet He was still protecting me.

In my post-degree courses, I was doing well. I was favored by lecturers and the Head of Section was even invited to watch me as I was scheduled to make a class presentation. I was like, "God, why are You so good to me?"

I was expecting to fail; I expected God to punish me for not having anything to do with Him.

I started seeking a church away from my home church and denomination where I could be restored and come back to God without judgment if I shared my struggles, sins, and challenges. I wanted to be healed without the distraction of people's comments on things being my fault and so on. I started wanting to pray again and reconnect with God. His goodness was reassuring me that He had not cast me away and that there was still hope. All I was seeking after would not give me the joy and fulfilment I longed for.

I needed God. During this time, I realized even more what it meant when we sang in church: Nothing else can take the place of feeling God's embrace. In all my experiences, the words of the Bible—that was just words to me in the past that I believed because God said it—became more meaningful to me as I experienced them.

CHAPTER SIX

THE JOURNEY OF HEALING BEGAN

I was invited to a prayer breakfast (a church event where people dine over breakfast and pray about issues), and I met a woman who invited me to a weekly prayer meeting at a church. I opted to go, saying that it was possibly my opportunity to be among people who are seeking after God, to find a safe space to be delivered from all the sins I have piled up, and to restore my relationship with God. God led her to mentor me and walk me through some things that would see me placing more value on myself and re-establishing my desire to be whole.

This was a divine connection. I did not realize I had entertained so many negative thoughts about myself and my life, and it had become a stronghold affecting every area of life: relationships, growth and personal development, and confidence to launch out and aspire for greater things.

After this mentorship ended, I engaged in counselling sessions to complete what God had started through my mentor. I had to rehearse some affirmations to replace the negative beliefs about myself that I had embraced. My self-esteem and how I viewed myself began to change. I no longer laid myself to be used to keep a relationship. I asserted my desires, stated where I disagreed with someone, and when I did not like something. Of course, people who were used to me being all cooperative, not asserting myself, and wanting to manipulate me would not be pleased with this change, but I had to now live for me and come out of the trap of pleasing others to gain their heart. People who truly love and respect you will want you to do the things that make you comfortable. It won't be a one-sided relationship.

On this journey, I was made aware that I magnified marriage to the point that I was willing to do anything to make it happen. I had to adjust my mindset and accept that whether it happens or not, I am still valuable.

During this journey of healing, I learned to cry out to God once I started struggling with sexual urges and when singleness became overbearing. God provided healthy relationships and activities that filled the gap for me because, truth be told, no relationship can replace that of an intimate relationship.

I started pursuing the passions and purpose in my heart and focused on them to keep me less preoccupied with being single and the struggles of not having a partner, seeing that I desired one.

CHAPTER SEVEN

THE ROAD TO MARRIAGE— FINALLY

When we walk in God's purpose, that is where miracles happen. Walking with God can lead to life-changing experiences.

I did not know that a young man at the new church I was attending had eyes on me. Like me, he was on a journey of processing and re-focusing and was now ending that journey to pursue a relationship.

We both felt a pull to attend a church activity one Saturday morning. This was the first day we sat and spoke undisturbed by crowd, as not many people turned up that day. We exchanged numbers, and the conversations began. Conversations led to dating. This was during COVID-19, so we were mostly online, and not many places were open for events.

There were times during dating when it felt like this was just another relationship that would not work out for me, but I found that each time something was interpreted a certain way, once we talked it through, it was clarified, and we were good again.

Then he proposed!

I was the chosen one, and I was honored to be. He was my chosen one, as I never had to compromise who I was or be someone I am not in order to feel loved.

CHAPTER EIGHT

CHURCH HURT

I had church hurt from very early in life as I grew up in the church as a pastor's kid (PK), and it complicated things for me. There were perks to being a PK. Some of them were easily getting recommendations, being in spaces where many top leaders/officials were, and receiving special treatment and privileges. All of this comes, especially when your parents are loved.

The hurts for me came in many forms. Some people were apparently jealous of these perks I would receive as a child, especially my own age group and gender. This got worse when it brought me attention from the opposite sex that other females would have wanted.

Another thing that would hurt was not being sure sometimes whether people were interested in me as a person when seeking out my company/friendship or if they really wanted to be in the company of their pastor, who was my father.

On the other hand, some would ill-treat me or speak grudgingly, and it was obvious that they did not like me.

I had to deal with all of this from an early age. I was just living my life, and things were coming to me that I never asked for, so why treat me badly because of it? On top of this, I was very talented and outgoing: a singer, dancer, assertive leader, and team player with bright ideas. This made me despised by those who just thought there was too much going on for me.

I started to suppress myself so that I didn't stand out so much and to avoid being disliked too much. As a teen, you are usually searching for your place and identity and just want to live and enjoy your youth, so this type of treatment coming from people at such an early age in life really made me sad. I struggled with identity, having to deal with people's expectations of how a pastor's kid should behave, dress, and carry themselves and the whole nine yards, and just learning who I am. I lived up to the expectations, but it was living in bondage because every time I wanted to do something for myself and to express me, I was always asking, "What will church people think?"

I was liberated outside of church circles when I met a vibrant group of young Christian women at university who wore their pants and jewelry and were dating guys for the purpose of marriage. They didn't look like the people of the traditional church I grew up in, where you had to wear long skirts and cover every part of your skin to be considered modest and holy. This experience at university drove home a liberating point for me: our relationship with God is not affected by what we wear and how we look but goes much deeper.

I started talking to my pastor, my dad, about the emphasis that is placed on wearing pants and jewelry, making people less of a Christian. When my dad saw my sister and I growing in God, even though we were starting to wear our pants and jewelry, he became convinced that external appearances do not need to be emphasized so much. He, however, did not place that personal belief or conviction on others. It was more for his household that he wanted to see modesty, so in respecting my dad, I ensured I wore my pants and jewelry modestly enough. Deep down, though, my conviction was that I could have double piercings in my ears, the biggest earrings, and wear shorts, which would not be a big deal with my relationship with God.

I had some unconventional convictions that I felt were too far-fetched from what the church would be comfortable with, so I suppressed who I really was to fit in the current status quo. Someone recognized my convictions were different, and someone said I should make sure I do not turn out to be the black sheep in my family. This statement lingered with me for a while and made me doubt from an early age that I could hear God for myself and that I probably wasn't fully saved. I thought I had to look to someone who seemed closer to God to know what His will was because I was not righteous enough to hear God for myself.

Hurts can be subtle and have a slow and negative effect over time if not dealt with.

One day, I got a word of prophecy that my life was going to draw others to Christ. This was someone who was very serious about serving God and spoke words that came to pass before, so I realized God spoke to them even about other people, and they were so on point.

This was a turning point for me in a spiritual sense. God knew my internal struggles and that I needed that encouragement. I started desiring to know God more, hear His voice for myself, and seek out the ways He wanted to use my life to draw people to Him.

Although I grew up reading the Word, praying, leading worship, and engaging in all kinds of ministries, other aspects of me outside of the spiritual needed attention. I realize we can be involved in ministry but not be a whole person in our everyday lives and relationships. I was hurt by the things people did and said to me. That put a limit on my growth.

I recall an experience where I was at a church event where people were joining a long line to serve food. I joined the line as well. I was curious as to what was being served, so I walked to the front of the line. Someone saw me appear at the front of the line and told me that I would not get any special treatment because I was a pastor's daughter and had to join the line like everyone else. This put a dagger in my heart. I was so young and pure in my heart and intentions, and to know that my actions were misjudged and mean things were said to me from as early as my teenage years really injured me emotionally.

After going through my healing journey, I saw the vast difference in how I came out confidently and was no longer hindered by what people thought or said about me. I decided that I needed to live my life to the max for me and not be bound to people anymore. I walk with self-esteem and confidence as a child of a King. How I view myself has changed. I transformed my mindset according to what God says about me. I am valuable. I deserve to live and exist like everyone else, so when people use their words and opinions to try to kill my spirit, I quickly reject them and reflect on what God has said about me.

Contrary to what some may think, after my dad stepped down from pastoral ministry, I considered myself to be a normal person and no longer a PK, even though I am an adult. I realized I had to work on the thought that my significance was not based on my status as a PK or my affiliation with my dad.

This change allowed me to feel okay because my self-worth was no longer based on my affiliations or the positions I held in church.

CHAPTER NINE

HURT IN THE CORPORATE WORLD

I have worked in several places and departments in my lifetime. In the corporate world, I also experienced being told hurtful things as a young lady just coming out of university and entering the working world with youthful exuberance.

At one of my early jobs, I was told by a senior lady that my type of degree did not have any place in the field of work I was trying to enter. It was a dagger. I was just trying to set up my life as an ambitious young lady. I shared the comment made with my mentor at the time, and she pushed me to enroll in a program that would qualify me for the field of work. I let that hurtful comment drive me to get the requisite certificate I needed rather than demotivate me.

In other instances, I was made to feel like people had my best interest at heart. They would ask how I was doing and about my life goals. I was new to the corporate world and not aware that people do feel threatened by new employees and sometimes feel insecure about their jobs in the workplace. I experienced being moved from high positions to lower-level positions without it being discussed with me or without being prepared for the change. I also experienced being sent home after a decision was made to terminate my contract and choose another staff member to do the job instead of me. I experienced deception, where lies were told on me to say I said something I did not say.

THE PURPOSE FOR THE STRUGGLES

Through all of these hurtful experiences in the corporate world, God had His hands in it. It appeared as if people were taking action and doing things that affected me negatively, but if that was not what God wanted for me, He would not have allowed it. It was God taking me to different places and positions throughout my life to work for short periods just to acquire the requisite knowledge and skills He knew I would need for the permanent job I was praying for.

When I shared my desire to land a permanent job, someone said that companies are not hiring permanent staff anymore, but I challenged God with His Word and reminded Him that He said, "If we ask, we will receive." (see Matthew 7:7). I prayed that prayer day and night. Then, one day, while working in a contract job, I got the call for a permanent position one year after doing the interview. God reminded me that it was what I had been praying for, so even though my current job seemed difficult to leave, He had opened that door for me, and I should go for it. So, I did.

When I started the job, and I went through the various job tasks, I was like, "God, You not easy at all." What I thought were negative experiences, God turned them all out for my good. Everything I learned in all my short-term jobs made me a very resourceful person to my employer.

I don't understand why God had to take me around the world in struggling to bring me into purpose, but I see how the struggles I went through benefitted me. When I quote the scripture, "All things work together for good to them that love God and are called to his purpose" (Romans 8:28 - KJV), I really believe it because I have experienced it.

In every short-term work experience I had, I acquired some new knowledge and skills that, when I finally settled and landed a permanent position, were instrumental to that job. I was such an asset that people consulted with me and had me influence managerial decisions. I quickly became grateful for how God used those seemingly bad experiences to benefit me. He did not want to position me and then have me struggling to perform at a job I had been waiting for, so He sent me where He knew I would grow, not only in terms of technical skills, but also my soft skills, such as leadership, negotiation and where I was forced to build persistence, strength and people skills.

In terms of intimate relationships, God had to mess things up when He saw I was not ready. I could not see how seriously my self-esteem would have affected any relationship I went into, so God had to pull me aside and keep me in singleness to address it. He connected me with a mentor to achieve this. I am forever grateful for this divine connection and the sacrifice they extended in ministering, praying, and mentoring me.

My husband, Adrian, is the image of God's love to me. I was not perfect when we were dating, but I was loved despite my imperfections. God was continuing His healing, even in my marriage, and showed me that I was going to give up a good and perfect gift that He had for me to be in relationships in the past where I would end up being unhappy.

Many women are sitting in compromising relationships because they do not believe there is anything better out there or that they will find anything better. You are giving up your full potential and dreams to appease someone who does not value you or what you have to offer.

I implore you to seek God and let Him lead you. This is not to say that sometimes we won't have to give up some things for the sake of a relationship that both individuals discuss and agree on; that is totally different.

CONCLUSION

Don't stay broken!

Whatever the source of your hurt, be it family, church, or corporate, you can be healed and whole again.

You can speak with a therapist, but I found that Jesus is the one who really makes you whole.

Don't delay today if you don't know Him as your Lord and Savior. He will be your joy, peace, and source of contentment throughout any circumstance in your life. He will make you whole again no matter what life brings your way.

www.ingramcontent.com/pod-product-compliance
Lightning Source LLC
LaVergne TN
LVHW051205080426
835508LV00021B/2819